What Happens Next?

DEALING WITH LIFE CHANGES

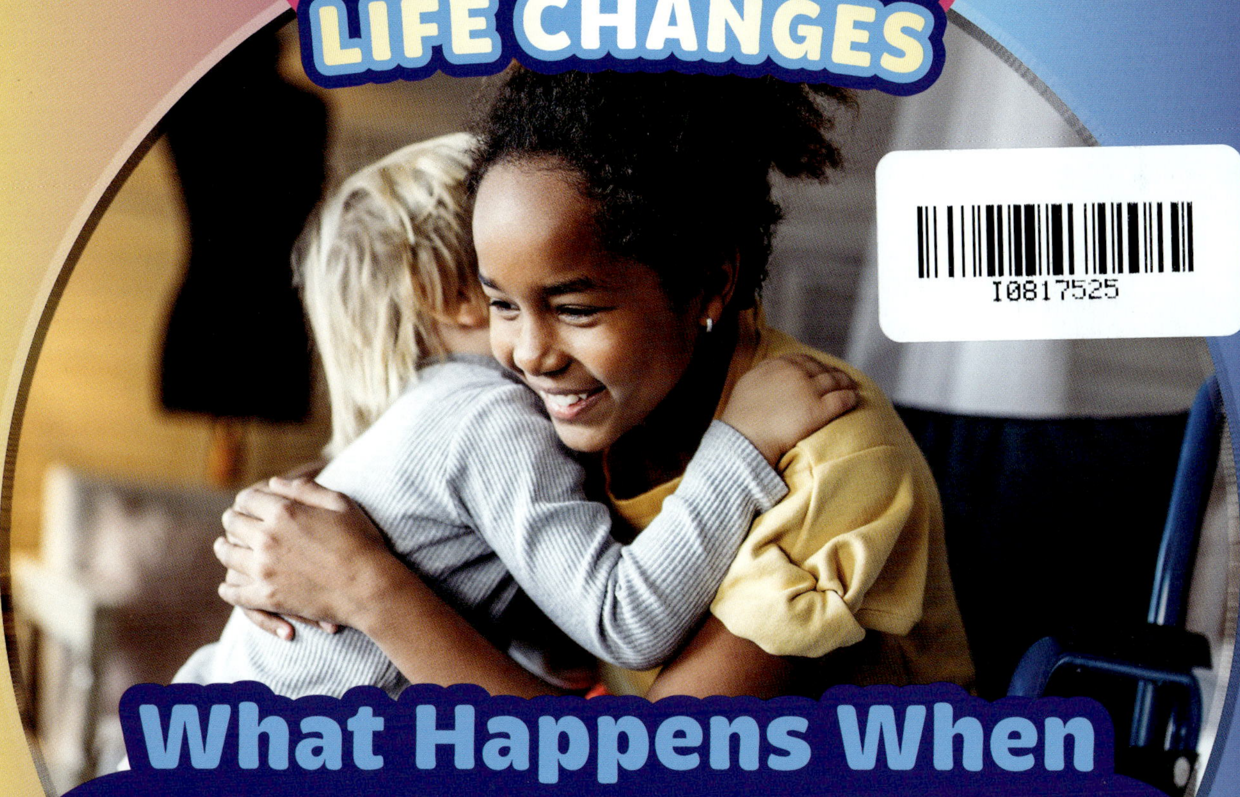

What Happens When I Have to Use a Wheelchair?

Kathleen A. Klatte

Published in 2025 by The Rosen Publishing Group, Inc.
2544 Clinton Street, Buffalo, NY 14224

First Edition

Editor: Theresa Emminizer
Book Design: Leslie Taylor

Photo Credits: Cover NDAB Creativity/Shutterstock.com; pp. 5, 9, 13, 21 wavebreakmedia/Shutterstock.com; p. 7 ROMSVETNIK/Shutterstock.com; p. 11 Tyler Olson/Shutterstock.com; p. 15 Prostock-studio/Shutterstock.com; p. 17 Africa Studio/Shutterstock.com; p. 19 AnnGaysorn/Shutterstock.com.

Cataloging-in-Publication Data

Names: Klatte, Kathleen A.
Title: What happens when I have to use a wheelchair? / Kathleen A. Klatte.
Description: Buffalo, NY : PowerKids Press, 2025. | Series: What happens next? dealing with life changes| Includes glossary and index.
Identifiers: ISBN 9781725327252 (pbk.) | ISBN 9781725327276 (library bound) | ISBN 9781725327283 (ebook)
Subjects: LCSH: Children with disabilities–Juvenile literature. | Wheelchairs–Juvenile literature.
Classification: LCC HV903.K525 2025 | DDC 362.4'3–dc23

Manufactured in the United States of America

Some of the images in this book illustrate individuals who are models. The depictions do not imply actual situations or events.

CPSIA Compliance Information: Batch #CSPK25. For Further Information contact Rosen Publishing at 1-800-237-9932.

CONTENTS

Freewheeling

People of all ages use wheelchairs. Sometimes it's just for a little while, because they've been sick or had an **accident**. Other people use a wheelchair all the time.

Your wheelchair is a very important tool. You use it to keep yourself safe and get where you need to go. While it's not the same as walking, you can use your wheelchair to get pretty much anywhere. You can go to school, stores, and parks. You can play sports and games!

Your Point of View

You might have heard about the Americans with Disabilities Act (ADA). This is an important national law. It says that public places must be **accessible** to people who use wheelchairs.

Your wheelchair is a tool that helps you go places and have fun with other kids!

Everyday Things

You might need to do some things differently because you use a wheelchair. There are many tools available to help.

Your home might look a bit different from your friends' homes, especially if you use a wheelchair all the time. There might be ramps, or slopes that join two surfaces, to help you move around more easily. Your house may have grab bars in the bathroom. You might also have a special chair so you can take a shower.

Your Point of View

Some big stores carry clothing designed, or made, to be comfortable for kids who use wheelchairs. Some of the first pieces were designed by moms. You might even see a model in an ad who looks just like you!

Some buses have lifts for wheelchairs. Your family might also get a van that's specially designed for your wheelchair.

Your Team

You probably have a team of people, including doctors and nurses, whose job is to help you stay safe and healthy. They probably will help you learn to use your wheelchair in new ways too.

You may visit different kinds of doctors. An orthopedist is a doctor who treats bones and muscles, or the parts of the body that allow movement. A physical therapist is a person who helps you with exercises to keep you strong. They also show you how to move safely.

An occupational therapist is someone who helps you learn how to do everyday things. They can show you how to do things such as getting dressed or reaching for things without falling.

Going to the Hospital

There will probably be times you need to go to the hospital. You might go to the **pediatric** ward of a local hospital, or you might go to a hospital that's just for kids. A hospital might seem scary at first, but sometimes it's the best place to find doctors who can help you.

There are people at the hospital whose job is to explain things so you and your family understand what's happening. You're always allowed to ask questions.

Your Point of View

In an **emergency**, your family and your medical team might need to make decisions quickly. This can be scary, but always remember that they're doing their best to help you.

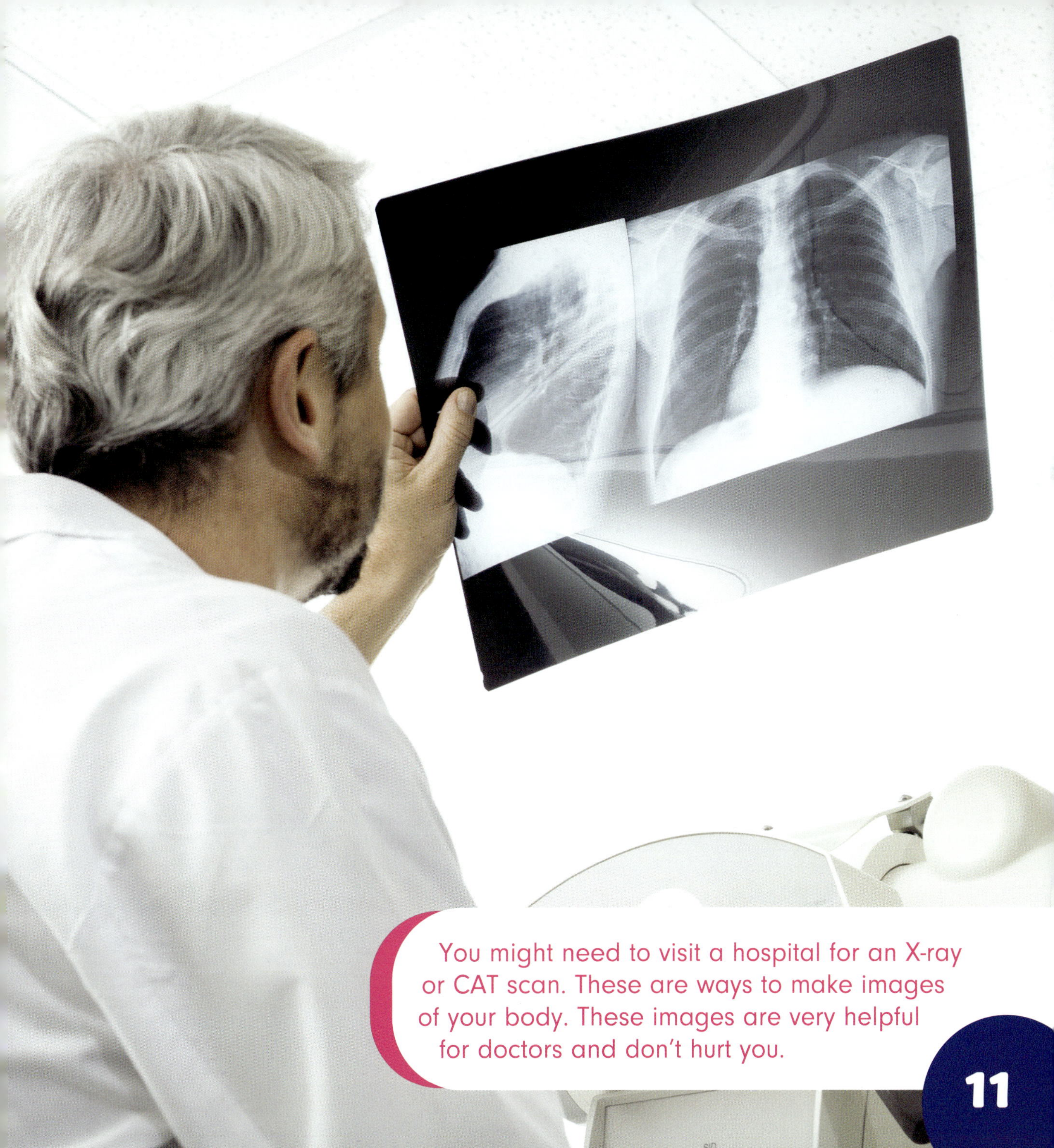

You might need to visit a hospital for an X-ray or CAT scan. These are ways to make images of your body. These images are very helpful for doctors and don't hurt you.

Going to School

All kids have to go to school! There are **federal** laws in the United States that say schools need to accommodate, or provide what's needed for, kids who use wheelchairs or other medical aids to get around. This means your school must have ramps and doors wide enough for your wheelchair. It also means there must be accessible bathrooms.

Yes, you still have to do homework! You're probably in a class with other kids your age and take all the same tests.

Your Point of View

If you have to stay in the hospital for a while, you'll still have to do schoolwork. Many large children's hospitals have classrooms and teachers to help you keep up with your class at home.

Kids who use wheelchairs can usually go to their neighborhood school with their friends.

Your Personal Space

Your wheelchair is part of your personal space. No one should touch it or you without your permission. Sometimes there will be people whose job it is to help you. They should always tell you who they are and explain what they're doing before they touch you or your wheelchair.

It's OK to say things like: "I can manage by myself, thank you." You can also ask for help with certain things: "Could you please hold that door for me?"

Your physical therapist will talk to you about what kind of exercises you're going to do and what they're trying to help you with.

Play Ball!

Did you know that lots of kids who use wheelchairs play sports? Many sports are **adapted** for kids who use wheelchairs or made just for you. You can play different ball games, or you can race. You might even try a sport like archery—shooting a bow and arrows!

You might be able to **compete** in sporting events. U.S. Paralympics is a group that runs competitions and **encourages** people who use wheelchairs or other adaptations to take part in sports.

Trying new sports is a great way to have fun and meet other kids.

Just for Fun

By law, public places in the United States have to be accessible for people who use wheelchairs. This doesn't just mean places you need to go, such as school. It also means places you want to go, such as parks and movie theaters.

Zoos and parks often make an extra effort to make sure everyone has a great time. In addition to ramps, they might include special viewing areas so that people who use wheelchairs can see everything.

Remember, your wheelchair is your freedom! It's a tool you use to explore the world and have fun.

Keep on Rolling!

Sometimes people don't know how to talk to someone who uses a wheelchair. They may be **insensitive** or act like they think you can't understand them. Smiling and saying hello can help. Offering to shake hands is a good way to get people to look at you and not your wheelchair.

Your wheelchair is a tool you use to learn and explore. You can do just about anything you put your mind to. So, keep on rolling!

Your Point of View

Other people should get on your level when they talk to you. If they don't, ask them politely. They might not have thought of it and be happy you asked.

Where will your wheelchair take you next?

Glossary

accessible: Able to be reached, approached, or used.

accident: A sudden event (such as a crash or fall) that isn't planned and that causes damage or injury.

adapt: To change to suit conditions.

compete: To try to get or win something.

emergency: An unexpected and usually dangerous situation that calls for immediate action.

encourage: To inspire with hope or courage.

federal: Relating to the central government of the United States.

insensitive: Showing that you do not know or care about the feelings of other people.

pediatric: Of or relating to the medical care or illnesses of children.

For More Information

Books

Cocca-Leffler, Maryann, and Janine Leffler. *We Want to Go to School!: The Fight for Disability Rights*. Park Ridge, IL: Whitman, Albert & Company, 2021.

Ladau, Emily. *Demystifying Disability: What to Know, What to Say, and How to Be an Ally*. Berkeley, CA: 10 Speed Press, 2021.

Websites

CDC
www.cdc.gov/ncbddd/kids/mobility.html
Check out the Kids' Quest page about mobility to learn more about living with a wheelchair.

Kids Health
kidshealth.org/en/kids/wheelchairs.html
Learn more about life in a wheelchair!

Index